WEALTH ON PURPOSE

STUDENT'S EDITION

Copyright © 2014 by J. Marcellas Williams
All Rights Reserved

No part of this book may be reproduced in any form without permission from the publisher, except in the case of brief quotations embodied in critical article of reviews.

ISBN-13: 978-1495388576
ISBN-10: 1495388573

All Scripture quotations are taken from Bible Gateway. Web. 25 Oct. 2012.

Printed in the United States of America

Foreword

Although we live in a day and season where fiscal concerns and financial subjects seem to dominate the front pages of the Wall Street Journal, USA Today and many other prominent periodicals, the Body of Christ is not worried, but preparing itself for the great wealth of God. Reason, there are no famines in the kingdom of God's people. Specifically, since we see financial challenges as an opportunity for God to express and manifest His wonders among us ~ the people of God. Our fiduciary responsibilities will be met as a result of seed sowing, budgeting and wise spending habits that are preached, taught and strongly emphasized from our pulpits and mid-week services. No longer does the twenty-first century church teach/preach the traditional sermons, but we are mindful to insert the everyday operational principles that are necessary for a whole means of living and progression.

The Word of God declares it is He who gives us the power to get wealth, thus Christians are determined and convinced that all of our answers are documented in the Holy Writ, and our directives are hidden in the golden nuggets of the Scriptures. Wealth is laced all throughout biblical text and mentioned as "...*money answereth all things*" (Eccl. 10:19).

As a twenty-first century warrior springing forth with knowledge, Pastor J. Marcellas Williams presents the wealth of God for the Body of Christ in practicality and easy written form. He shares principles of wealth, personal testimonies and strategies for our current day and future in the prosperity of God.

Our days of poverty are over and done with due to our knowledge of the wealth in God's divine principles. As members of the Christian faith we are encouraged and challenged to tithe, sow seed, give offerings and first fruits according to the Scriptures, and it is all done via faith and obedience. This book "WEALTH ON PURPOSE" highlights that your present and future riches are not just a "pie in the sky", but a direct lineage to your practice of God's curriculum that will set our journey toward the continuance of God's financial blessing.

Set your mindset for greatness and plan your agenda for success on various levels, but it will only happen when you take time to read, digest and study written materials like this published work that will guide you in the ideology of God's wealth. MONEY KNOWS MONEY AND IS COMING IN OUR DIRECTION.

Bishop Eric D. Garnes, D. Min, MPS
Presiding Prelate, United Covenant Churches of Christ
Senior Pastor, Tabernacle of Praise (Cathedral)
Brooklyn, New York

Table of Contents

1. **Salutation**...6

2. **Wealth on Purpose Confession**..............................8

3. **Overview**..9

4. **8 Laws of Wealth**...10

5. **Testimonial**..11

6. **7 On Purpose Steps**...13

7. **First Fruit**...16

8. **Testimonial**..18

9. **Tithe** 19

10. **8 Fold Blessing from Tithe and Offering**.........20

11. **Kingdom Giving**..21

12. **Top 10 Reasons People Do Not Tithe**.................22

13. **Testimonial**..23

14. **Quick Review**..25

15. **Shepherd's Seed**..26

16. **Alms Giving**...27

17. **Testimonials**..28

18. **Notes**..33

Salutation

Greetings,

Thank you for supporting and investing into J. Marcellas Ministries and into your own life and ministry. What an honor to be used by God as a vessel to compose this handbook. The greatest revelry for me is to hear the countless testimonies that have been birthed as a result of God's people applying the principles shared within this handbook. The first testimony came from my own struggles that were turned into victories. By using these principles I live a debt free life enjoying the wealth of God in every area of my life. I will also be the first to say although the principles and teachings in this handbook are simple and easy to understand and apply, habits are hard to break. Bad habits are broken when bad thinking is fixed. This handbook will challenge and cause a change from bad thinking to thinking God's way as it relates to finances.

I serve as the pastor and founder of Life Church International of Jacksonville, Florida. God has blessed the LCI family tremendously since its inception in 2007. I also serve as the Adjutant Chaplain to the Presiding Bishop of the United Covenant Churches of Christ, Bishop Eric D. Garnes. My most joyful and rewarding area of service I render as unto God is being a husband to my wife and a father to my children. I am proudly married to Marquita Denise Williams since October 1, 2006. She is my rock and my love. She is my parenting partner to our three children, Navah Simone, Jade Michelle and Marcellas Dominic.

Once more, thank you for your support. I am excited about your future. Be sure to pray and seek God before and while reading and working through this handbook. Ask God to speak to you and reveal to you his Word and instructions for your life through this work.

Pastor J.

Testimonial

You may have read books or attended conferences on the topic before--but not like this one. **"Wealth On Purpose"** is not just an instruction manual. It is a pastor's recommendation on how to assess your wealth using qualities that are neglected by many Christians today. Through these teachings that I've been privy to sit under and learn as a pastor myself, I have seen them work if they are properly adhered to and applied. I've seen and heard the testimonies of persons who have diligently walked out these principles. Lives have been changed and made better financially only after becoming good stewards over what God has already given. The Word of God is true....He has given us the power to get wealth (Deut. 8:18). This is foundational teaching in which I highly recommend. This teaching belongs in the hands of every person, especially every believer who seeks and prays for financial reformation. It's a MUST!!!!

Curtis C. Johnson

Founder-Pastor, The Perfecting Saints Church, Jacksonville, Fl.

God takes pleasure in my prosperity! Therefore, the cycle of poverty has been broken from my life. I have financial discipline. God can trust me with wealth. I no longer live with holes in my pockets. For I have blessed pockets and I live in wealth on purpose! In Jesus name, Amen!

Wealth on Purpose

5 Principles of Giving

1) _____

2) _____

3) _____

4) _____

5) _____

4 Steps to Wealth

1) _____

2) _____

3) _____

4) _____

8 Laws of Wealth

Law 1: _____
Now the One who provides **seed for the sower** and bread for food will provide and multiply your seed and increase the harvest of your righteousness. *2 Corinthians 9:10*

Law 2: _____
Give, and it shall be given unto you; good measure, pressed down, and shaken together, and running over, shall men give into your bosom. For with the same measure that ye mete withal it shall be measured to you again. *Luke 6:38*

Law 3: _____
Remember this: The person who **sows** sparingly will also **reap** sparingly, and the person who sows generously will also reap generously. *2 Corinthians 9:6*

Law 4: _____
Then he that had received the five talents went and traded with the same, and made them other five talents. *Matthew 25:16*

Law 5: _____
The rich rule over the poor, and the **borrower is servant to the lender**. *Proverbs 22:7*

Law 6: _____
The wicked borrow and do not repay, but the righteous **give generously** *Psalm 37:21*

Law 7: _____
Let no debt remain outstanding, except the continuing debt to love one another, for he who loves his fellowman has fulfilled the law. *Romans 13:6-8*

Law 8: _____
Keep your lives free from the love of money and **be content with what you have**, because God has said, "Never will I leave you; never will I forsake you. *Hebrews 13:5*

Testimonial

My wife, Beverly and I, are two former crack addicts as well as former U.S. Postal workers who were terminated in the late 80's. Back then, if you worked for the Post Office you were considered as having a "premium" job. During this time we were considered what was called "functioning addicts' meaning we would smoke drugs and get high but still go to work when we were supposed to, but pay day was a different story altogether. We had a slogan we used for our Friday pay days - "money in hand, change in plan". We would spend practically every penny of our paychecks and be broke on Saturday. This vicious cycle went on for quite some time until we both eventually were terminated from our company. No one believed that we would ever overcome our addictions or have any material things of life again. But thanks to the prayers of our mothers, and many others, God was still working in our lives.

The first time I heard the terms "First Fruits" and "Shepherd's Seed" was after I had become a member of Life Church International. Pastor J was teaching on these topics and I know it had to be God that led me there because my purpose for going was to stop my wife from going, which she had already become a member. However, all that changed once I stepped inside the doors of the sanctuary. I was greeted with much love and affection. I was unemployed at the time, and Pastor J taught a message entitled "Better". Shortly after that I was re-hired by the company that fired me. Then came the message "Prepare for the Rain", which made me feel like he was speaking directly to me. That caused me to step out on faith and start my very own trucking business. The next teaching that came was "Learning How to Hear from God". During this teaching the church was put on a fast and I believe God spoke to me to expand the business and for us to purchase a second truck. Shortly after that, I got confirmation by way of my wife being terminated from her job of 18 years. Then, immediately the second truck was purchased with only half of what used to be a two income household. God's still working!

Now comes the teaching of "First Fruits" and "Shepherd's Seed", where Pastor J taught us how the Levites took care of the Shepherd with the first fruits of their harvest to cover them for the remainder of the year. This started as a struggle in our flesh because it was also time to file our taxes, and we had not put any money aside if we had to pay the IRS. We decided that we were going to be obedient to God and the teachings and pay our first fruits, which was a huge sacrifice. We got our taxes filed, and not only did we not have to pay, but we got a tremendous blessing of a $21,000.00 refund. God's principles of Tithing, Offerings, First Fruits, and Shepherd's Seed are for our benefit that truly work and are available to anyone who is willing to apply the principles. There is no pit too low that God can't raise you up and out of. To God be the Glory.

In His service,
Howard Hooper

7 On Purpose Steps

J. Marcellas Williams

On Purpose Step 1 - _____

A rainy day kitty is for those unexpected events where you need quick cash. These events happen suddenly and call for immediate action. For example, a pipe bursts at home, your transmission goes out in the car, or you have to take an emergency trip out of town due to a loved one being sick, etc. No one is exempt from these costly rainy day events from occurring. It is a matter of *when* not if.

This rainy day kitty will serve as a buffer to borrowing for such emergencies, which causes you to go deeper in debt. No more borrowing. It's time to break the cycle of debt and poverty!

START NOW!

On Purpose Step 2 – _____

Create a checklist of your debts. Start with the smallest balance and work your way up to the largest. Don't worry about interest rates unless two debts have similar payoffs. If that's the case, then list the higher interest rate debt first.

The Debt Demolishing System creates momentum by giving you quick and frequent victories. These victories will motivate you to keep going. After a while the large bills will not seem so intimidating any longer. The same amount that you have allotted to pay of the first debt adds to the next debt. Then take those two monthly allotted amounts and add to the next debt. Continue this trend and by the time you reach the larger debts you will be able to tackle it more aggressively. **START NOW!**

7 On Purpose Steps

On Purpose Step 3 - _____

Determine what it costs for you to live for a total of three to six months. That will serve as the amount to save for your cushion fund. Use the same money that was allotted to pay your debts off in the previous step for this fund. Utilize this money for emergencies only especially, for situations that would cause a decrease in your monthly household income. I recommend that you keep these savings in a money market account. **START NOW!**

On Purpose Step 4 - _____

Congratulations, by now you should have no payments (except the house) and a fully funded rainy day kitty. Now we want to work on creating extra streams of income and becoming aggressive about our retirement fund.

Research and find a business, stock or personal venture that you can invest in. Start small and work your way up. It would be foolish to invest all of your extra money. In addition, I recommend investing no less than 10% of your household income into Roth IRAs and pre-tax retirement plans. **START NOW!**

> **"Money is like a sixth sense – and you can't make use of the other five without it."**
>
> **- William Somerset Maugham**

> **"Virtue does not come from wealth, but. . . wealth, and every other good thing which men have. . . comes from virtue." - Socrates**

7 On Purpose Steps

J. Marcellas Williams

On Purpose Step 5 – _____

Attaining a college degree is possible without having to acquire loans. Set a goal that would adequately satisfy the money needed for college. Determine how much per month you should be saving at 12% interest in order to have enough for college. If you save at 12% and inflation is at 4%, then you are moving ahead of inflation at a net of 8% per year! I recommend using Education Savings Accounts (ESAs) and 529 plans to save for college. **START NOW!**

On Purpose Step 6 – _____

You still have extra money but don't quite look at it as extra yet. We will call it unmarked money instead. Use this money to aggressively pay off your mortgage early. You have built up a massive force of momentum so don't slow down now. You are just about at the dream of having no debt. *Romans 13:6-8* **START NOW!**

On Purpose Step 7 – _____

You are now living in abundance. Allow God to use you to bless others. Be generous because giving as God leads can never deplete you. God always gives back more than what we give. Also, be certain to leave an inheritance for your family.

Be careful not to get all you can, can all you get and then sit on the can. Vow to never hold your money so tightly that you never give any away. Hoarding money is a sign of fear. Giving is a sign of faith. **START NOW!**

5 Principles of Giving

First Fruit

J. Marcellas Williams

1) **First Fruit**

2) Tithe

3) Shepherd's Seed

4) Kingdom Giving

5) Alms Giving

Hebrew meaning: _____

Greek meaning: _____

Principle: If the _____ is blessed the _____ is blessed (Romans 11:16 KJV)

Purpose: Honor the Lord _____ and He shall fill you with _____ until it overflows (Proverbs 3:9-10 GWT)

Prohibition: Don't _____ with it. It is _____ to the Lord (Ezekiel 48:14)

Place: In the house of _____ (Exodus 23:19)

Priest: _____

    Ezekiel 44:30 – The _____ shall cause the _____ to rest in your house

    2 Chronicles 31:4 – Helps to keep your _____ encouraged

Practice: It consists of a fourth of your monthly income. This amount is to be presented to God at the beginning of the year.

    Your Pay - $1000 per month / by 4 =

    Your First fruit - $250

When you receive a steady raise in your income, you are to give God the first of the raise.

    Your Raise – $100 more per month / by 4 =

    Your First fruit - $25

5 Principles of Giving

Harvesting is the process of _____ mature crops from the field. The harvest marks the _____ of the growing cycle. On smaller farms with minimal mechanization, harvesting is the _____ labor intensive activity of the growing season. On large, mechanized farms, harvesting utilizes the _____ expensive and sophisticated farm machinery. There are a number of _____ required after removing the crops: cooling, sorting, cleaning, packing, processing and shipping.

When God blesses you with a harvest it requires you to take responsible action. We show God we are grateful or ungrateful by the type of steward we are.

Hindrance – But seek ye _____ the _____, and his _____: and all these things shall be added unto you. Matthew 6:33

- Know the _____ of the Kingdom of God
- Trust the _____ of the Kingdom
- _____ according to His ways
- _____ all these things will be added

Testimonial

Hello Pastor J!

I am writing to share my progress and testimony regarding the 5 principles of giving. First, I just want to say, I thank God for leading me to Life Church international. You, Lady M and the whole LCI Family have been a blessing to me and my family.

Well, I have been tithing for a while. However, my overall attitude regarding giving has changed and that's a testimony in itself. My biggest issue was with First Fruits. I was nervous because the amount of one week's pay is well more than I have ever given at one time. Even though I felt that way, I said with my mouth that I choose to Trust GOD in my finances knowing that some kind of way all my needs will be met. So, I set my mind to make sure I just take the money out and put it straight into the envelope and seal it. In the same week, a series of things began to happen.

1. An overflow of loans hit our department, my manager personally asked me to work extra hours even though I didn't qualify yet because I was new. So, even after the first fruit seed I had money for my bills.

2. At the beginning of the school year, my oldest son Tony was denied the grant for free tutoring services, so I have been looking for a company that provides tutoring for a reasonable price. I was planning to start tutoring services this week. But one day during lunch I was checking my voicemail and got a message from a tutoring company that says they were calling because they got information from Duval County Schools to start tutoring Tony. So Tony has free tutoring for at least 90 days from the same company that gave me a rate of $40.00 an hour.

3. Recently, I became a Florida Notary. God opened the door for me to be the personal notary for a tax company. I only go there once a week for no more than 2 hours. For the past 2 weeks, I have made more in those couple hours than I do in a whole days work on my job and I just say Thank You Jesus, for providing all my needs and above my needs.

I am learning to trust GOD in all things and I know he will give me the wisdom I need to succeed in every area. My motivational scripture:

Philippians 3:13 Brethren, I count not myself to have apprehended: but [this] one thing [I do], forgetting those things which are behind, and reaching forth unto those things which are before, 14 I press toward the mark for the prize of the high calling of God in Christ Jesus.

Thank you,

Chauna S. White

5 Principles of Giving

Tithe / Kingdom Giving

J. Marcellas Williams

1) First Fruit

2) **Tithe**

3) Shepherd's Seed

4) **Kingdom Giving**

5) Alms Giving

Foundation: And _____ of the land, whether of the seed of the land, or of the fruit of the tree, is the Lord's: _____ unto the Lord. *Leviticus 27:30*

Example: Abram tithes to Melchizedek *Genesis 14:18-20*

Amount: Each year you are to set aside a _____ **(10%) of all the produce** grown in your fields. Deuteronomy 14:22

Purpose: 1) God desires a sincere heart to heart _____ between himself and his children.

God does not _____ our _____, He longs for our _____ and our _____.

2) God has designed the tithe to _____ the needs of the local _____

Malachi 3:6-7, Matthew 6:21

How it works: Tithing is a sign of _____, _____ and

_____ toward God. Tithing is our _____ service. Tithing affords us _____ but not complete fulfillment.

Malachi 3:8-12

*** ALL SAINTS STRIP CLUB ***

5 Principles of Giving

Tithe / Kingdom Giving

J. Marcellas Williams

8 Fold Blessing from Tithe and Offering

1) _____ of heaven are open to you

2) God will _____ _____ a blessing to you

3) The blessing will be in _____

4) Hold back the _____ from you

5) Your blessing shall not be _____

6) God will ensure you don't _____ prematurely

7) The glory/favor of God will _____ on you

8) People will _____ into your life perpetually

5 Principles of Giving

J. Marcellas Williams

Kingdom Giving

Rule: You must _____ in order to expect a _____ .

Give, and it shall be given unto you; good measure, pressed down, and shaken together, and running over, shall men give into your bosom. For with the same measure that ye mete withal it shall be measured to you again. *Luke 6:38*

Terms and Conditions: _____ control the rate of return

6Remember this: Whoever sows sparingly will also reap sparingly, and whoever sows generously will also reap generously. **7**Each man should give what he has decided in his heart to give, not reluctantly or under compulsion, for God loves a cheerful giver. **8**And God is able to make all grace abound to you, so that in all things at all times, having all that you need, you will abound in every good work. *2 Corinthians 9:6-8*

10Now he who supplies seed to the sower and bread for food will also supply and increase your store of seed and will enlarge the harvest of your righteousness. **11**You will be made rich in every way so that you can be generous on every occasion, and through us your generosity will result in thanksgiving to God.   *2 Corinthians 9:10-11*

Hinder: Your _____ and your _____ are essential to

God's _____ of your investment in the kingdom.

3And in process of time it came to pass, that Cain brought of the fruit of the ground an offering unto the LORD. **4**And Abel, he also brought of the firstlings of his flock and of the fat thereof. And the LORD had respect unto Abel and to his offering: **5**But unto Cain and to his offering he had not respect. And Cain was very wroth, and his countenance fell. **6**And the LORD said unto Cain, Why art thou wroth? and why is thy countenance fallen? **7**If thou doest well, shalt thou not be accepted? and if thou doest not well, sin lieth at the door. And unto thee *shall be* his desire, and thou shalt rule over him. **8**And Cain talked with Abel his brother: and it came to pass, when they were in the field, that Cain rose up against Abel his brother, and slew him. **9**And the LORD said unto Cain, Where *is* Abel thy brother? And he said, I know not: *Am* I my brother's keeper? Genesis 4: 3-9

5 Principles of Giving

Tithe / Kingdom Giving

J. Marcellas Williams

Top 10 Reasons People Do not Tithe

10. _____

9. They don't trust the _____

8. Poor _____ management

7. Believe that giving 10% of their _____ and _____ takes the

place of giving _____

6. Believe it is a money _____ concocted by the _____

5. Claims tithing have never _____ for them

4. Living from _____ to _____ is satisfactory

3. Fear of not having enough _____ to pay _____

2. No real _____ of the true meaning and purpose of tithing

1. They don't trust _____

"Money is like manure, its only good if you spread it around."

— Winston S. Churchill

"It is not the creation of wealth that is wrong, but the love of money for its own sake."

- Margaret Thatcher

Testimonial

Greetings Pastor J,

My husband and I have been applying the **Wealth On Purpose** principles and I would like to share with you a few things that God has done for me and my family. We began our journey here in Jacksonville in January 2007. I was fired from a job 3 months prior in September of 2006 (two days before our wedding day) and did not find work until February 2007. We stayed in a room in a relative's home for a few months before God opened the door for us to purchase our own home in April. August came around and I was told that because of budget cuts I could not return to work and due to financial difficulty at my husband's place of employment his pay suffered greatly. We did not know how we were going to eat day to day, how we were going to get our lights back on or how we were going to get around the city with little to no gas. Not to mention, our laundry and my hair was needed a relaxer, badly!!! We did not have air conditioning for the first few years of being in our new home. The summer months were difficult. We struggled for months until I was able to find temporary employment in October. Soon after, God provided me with permanent employment in February of 2008. I remained employed with this company until September 2012. I was stressed and bitter the majority of my tenure there. My hair was falling out, and the position I worked in was very stressful.

Nevertheless, throughout all of our struggles my husband and I NEVER turned our backs on God. We were in church faithfully, even when we didn't really want to be there. We served the church and others faithfully. We trusted and believed that God would bring us out of these day to day struggles. We continued to give of ourselves and whatever we possessed because we believed that if we continued to give-not grudgingly- that our hands would remain open for God to place blessings within them. Even though we did not have much we gave what we had. We paid our tithe from whatever came into our hands. God placed people in our lives to bless us at our lowest and darkest times. Even some people who schemed and plotted against us to keep us down God used them to bless us, his children.

Pastor, God has given you many sermons to share with us that have truly helped my husband and I understand him more. The instructions were so clear. They were simple and we knew that they would only be hard to follow if we didn't follow them. The 5 Principles of Giving and the 7 On Purpose Steps that God gave you to give to us at Life Church helped us and has been helping us become debt free and live in **wealth on purpose**. They have blessed us so....we have been applying these principles and denying our flesh (most of the time) and we have shared the messages with others and so far:

1. I have been blessed with a great paying career that embodies my occupation desires

2. My children have schools that are both affordable & dependable with 1 yr free tuition

3. My children are healthy and are now covered with an affordable insurance plan

4. My husband has been accepted into a program that will award him access to a career of his goals as an addition to his successful business he runs.

5. We received an unexpected lump sum check in the mail

6. Much of our debt has been demolished! We have a student loan and our house note remaining....

With love and appreciation,

Lisa

5 Principles of Giving

J. Marcellas Williams

1) First Fruit

2) Tithe

3) **Shepherd's Seed**

4) Kingdom Giving

5) **Alms Giving**

Quick Review

First Fruit
Principle: If the _____ is blessed the _____ is blessed *Romans 11:16 KJV*

Practice: It consists of a fourth of your monthly income. This amount is to be presented to God at the beginning of the year.

Tithe
Foundation: And _____ of the land, whether of the seed of the land, or of the fruit of the tree, is the Lord's: _____ unto the Lord. *Leviticus 27:30*

Kingdom Giving
Rule: You must _____ in order to expect a _____.

Give, and it shall be given unto you…*Luke 6:38*

~ 25 ~

5 Principles of Giving

Shephard's Seed / Alms Giving

J. Marcellas Williams

Shepherd's Seed

Resource: It is biblically supported that the _____ should be supported _____ by the church *1 Corinthians 9: 3-14*

Responsibility: It is a biblical response for the receivers of the Word to bless the giver of the Word. *Galatians 6: 6, 9*

Recipe: God is a _____ and _____ God.
The effect – God provides your needs.
The cause – you _____ the needs of your _____.

Every man according as he purposeth in his heart, so let him give; not grudgingly, or of _____: for God loveth a cheerful giver. *2 Corinthians 9:7,*

But my God shall supply all your _____ according to his riches in glory by Christ Jesus. *Philippians 4:19*

Your Pastor/Covering is _____ to you as a blessing to you as you are a _____ to them. *1Kings 17:9-17*

5 Principles of Giving

J. Marcellas Williams

Alms Giving

Formula: I have shewed you all things, how that so labouring ye ought to support the weak, and to remember the words of the Lord Jesus, how he said, **It is more blessed to _____ than to _____.** *Acts 20:35*

Giving to those who are less _____ is a _____ matter not to be broadcasted or _____.

Don't give with the motive of _____. Give because you have been _____ to give. Don't look for a reward from the person; _____ will reward you. *Matthew 6:1-4*

*** Take Action ***

Testimonial

I recently finished teaching on Alms Giving and I was shopping in a department store a few weeks later. I found some of the best sales and bargains on the few items I purchased. As I approached the counter to check out I read the name tag of the clerk that would assist me. She looked to be at least in her late fifties or early sixties.

"Hi Cindy, how are you today"? I said.

She replies, "Well I'm here, how are you"? We continued small talk, but her first reply, 'Well I'm here' made me tune in to our conversation a little more it caused me to become concerned. To lighten the conversation I joked with Cindy saying that my wife says I'm cheep.

Cindy said with a smile, "Next time tell her you are not cheap you just cut corners to have more money left over to spend on her." we both laughed.

Suddenly her demeanor changed and her facial expression dropped. She talked about how she had been married twice and she was done with believing in marriage altogether. She encouraged her daughter not to get married to her boyfriend that she is living with and has been dating for the last five years. She went as far as to advice her daughter to have children with him but not to marry him.

Cindy continued talking about how she has four children from her first husband. She said he treated so badly when they were married. She remembered how he expected her to keep the floors scrubbed, food prepared and on the table by six o'clock every night; take care of the children, work and take care of him. She was to do all of this with no help from him. She would ask her husband to help with the kids and he would snap at her and reply, "You wanted these kids so you take care of them!"

Even more disturbing she explained how her children were all grown now and she just exists now. She mentioned that she only goes to work and goes home. Cindy also stated, she now lives with her daughter because no one else wants to be bothered. To me she seemed depressed and bitter. So I asked her what advice she could give me for my marriage. She admonished me to show my wife that I care and consider her. Cindy urged me to buy my wife a card or flowers ever so often for no other reason but to show her you were thinking about her. "Those small acts of kindness go along way and can really brighten up her day." she counseled. I said, "Thank you and enjoy the rest of your day."

I walked away and another customer approached Cindy's register. The customer asked how she was today and Cindy again replied with a smile, "Well, I'm here." God began to speak to my spirit to do something nice for Cindy in order that He may minister to her. I heard the spirit instruct me to take the same advice she gave me for my wife and use it to brighten Cindy's day. I thought to buy her a card and give her a seed of $50. I honestly did not want to do anything but pray for her and move on. God would not allow this thought to leave me alone so I asked my wife if she was okay with me doing this for this woman. My wife was elated with the idea. Here is what the card read.

Hi Cindy, I was in your store the other day, we spoke briefly and you gave me great wisdom on how to be a better husband to my wife. I wanted to get you this card to say thank you. I noticed that you may be facing rough time in your life now, but things will get better for you. Be careful not to rely on any man for your happiness because every person in your life will disappoint you in some way. The only person who will never disappoint you is Jesus. I do not know if you know Him or not but if not please get to know him because He loves you more than you love yourself. Never stop smiling, it allows the light into your soul.

I placed the fifty dollars in the card along with my business card, just in case she wanted to get in touch with me to learn more about Christ or just to say thank you. I went by the store to drop the card off. I left it with one of her co-workers while she was on break. I did not want to really carry on a great conversation so I left. I knew this act of kindness was not about me I needed only to be obedient to God. It has been over two months since I did this and I have not received a response from Cindy, but God honored my obedience. Two weeks after I left the card my wife and I received an unexpected check in the mail for the amount of seventeen hundred dollars. God honored our obedience to him because we followed the principles of Alms Giving.

P.S. My wife and I remain in prayer for Cindy.

Signed:
Pastor J Marcellas

Testimonial

For about two years, my family and I have been faithful disciples of Life Church International. When Pastor J. initially began teaching the **"Wealth On Purpose"** series, I did not start applying the principles he taught. As I began to grow more I started applying the principles; my children and I *began seeing a difference in our finances*. My eleven year old son Kristopher, a fifth grade safety patrol officer at Martin Luther King Jr. Elementary School, really took notice.

Each year, the school's safety patrols take a trip to Washington DC to tour the monuments and see the sites. They also take a trip to Busch Gardens in Tampa at the end of the year. The total cost of these trips comes to $632.00, not including money for food and expenditures. Now, I'm a single parent and I'm not making that much on my job to be able to come up with this type of money by the end of the year, seeing that I have bills and other pressing matters. However, I thought to myself, 'this is a once in a life time trip!' What could I do to help my child? How could I come up with money, the right way and not the wrong way? Surprisingly, Kristopher came to me and said, "Mama, what would Pastor J say?" So, I replied "you're right!" Then, he said to me, "Mama, can you ask Pastor J would it be ok for me to sale some items after church to raise my funds for my trip?" I told him I would and so, I did. Pastor J permitted us to start selling. So every Sunday my son would go out in front of the church and sell his snack items. He was out there no matter what; in the hot sun, the cold wind, and sometimes in the dripping rain trying to raise that money for his trip.

During the weeks that Pastor J was teaching the **'Wealth On Purpose'** series, I instilled into Kristopher the principles and *he followed those steps*, including paying his tithe every week from the money he made by selling the snack items [Tithe]. He gave a seed offering toward the

Life City Vision [Kingdom Giving]. Furthermore, he gave Pastor J, his wife and kids a bag full

of chips, sodas, and candy every week for free [Sheppard's Seed]. All the while he was faithful,

being a good steward to his candy store. Pastor J had spoken to Kristopher and told him that he

would give $100 of his own money to help toward his trip. Well, Kristopher remembered Pastor

J spoke about giving and being a blessing to others. It just so happened that there was another

child at Life Church who was also a safety patrol officer, yet, at a different school, and they

wanted to also raise funds for the same trip. My son graciously stepped aside to let the other

child sell snack items so that this child could gain as much support as he did [Alms Giving].

What an awesome gesture of Godly love and being a blessing to others. Pastor J, however

remembered his promise to Kristopher and one Sunday he told the church our story. Just as he

finished telling the story Pastor J pulled out the $100 that he had previously told Kristopher he

would give him. He then, asks the other members to sow a seed into Kristopher for his trip.

With that being said, *my son is debt free!!* He paid for his trip and was blessed with

overflow: spending money for his trip. Hallelujah! This is something that we are totally thankful

for. Generosity never goes unnoticed! Kristopher was faithful to God, LCI, and his store and *God*

returned the faithfulness with interest!! Kris now wants to sale the rest of his snack items and

donate the money from those sales to the youth department at the LCI to go towards the 'Back 2

School' supplies. I am a very proud mother of a kindhearted young man. As long as he keeps

listening to the word of God that is being taught through our pastor, Pastor J. Marcellas

Williams, and applying these principles and 'Living On Purpose', my son will make it even

further than my mind can imagine. He will experience **'Wealth On Purpose'**!

Proud Mother,

Randesha Brown

Notes

Notes

Made in United States
Orlando, FL
03 March 2024